ECUADOR

MAJOR WORLD NATIONS
ECUADOR

Sarita Kendall

CHELSEA HOUSE PUBLISHERS
Philadelphia

Chelsea House Publishers

Copyright © 1999 by Chelsea House Publishers,
a division of Main Line Book Co.

Library of Congress Cataloging-in-Publication Data

Kendall, Sarita.
Ecuador / Sarita Kendall.
p. cm. — (Major world nations)
Includes index.
Summary: Explores the people, history, culture, land, climate, and
economy of Ecuador, which takes its name from the fact that the equator crosses
through its mountains just north of the capital city of Quito.
ISBN 0-7910-4970-1 (hc)
1. Ecuador—Juvenile literature. [1. Ecuador.] I. Title.
II. Series.
F3708.5.K46 1998
986.6—dc21   98-4341
CIP
AC

ACKNOWLEDGEMENTS

The author and publishers are grateful to the following organizations and individuals for
permission to reproduce copyright illustrations in this book:
S.C. Bisserot/Nature Photographers Ltd; Hilary Bradt/South American Pictures;
Michael Gore/Nature Photographers Ltd; M.P. Harris/Nature Photographers Ltd; John
Karmali/Nature Photographers Ltd; Marion and Tony Morrison/South American
Pictures; Timothy Ross.

4

CONTENTS

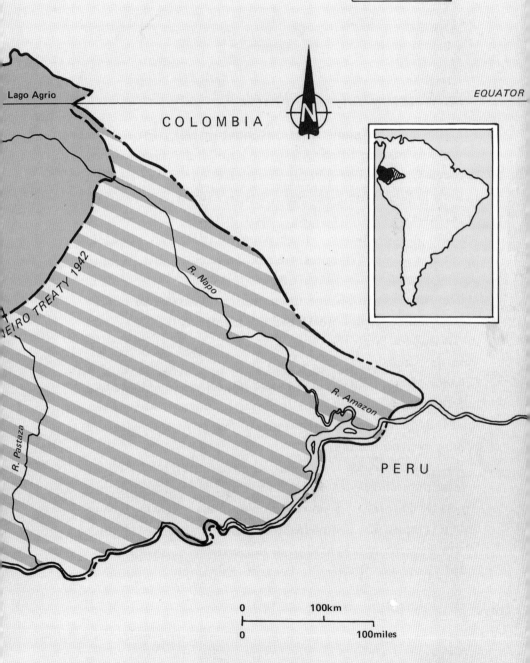

ECUADOR

Lago Agrio

EQUATOR

COLOMBIA

R. Napo

RIO DE JANEIRO TREATY 1942

R. Amazon

R. Pastaza

PERU

0   100km

0   100miles

FACTS AT A GLANCE

Land and People

Official Name	Ecuador
Location	Ecuador is located on the Pacific coast of South America, south of Colombia. The Galapagos Islands are located in the Pacific Ocean, 602 miles (970 kilometers) west of Ecuador.
Area	105,040 square miles (272,045 square kilometers)
Climate	Tropical with many climate variations due to ocean currents and mountainous regions
Capital	Quito
Other Cities	Guayaquil, Cuenco
Population	11.5 million
Population Density	105 persons per square mile
Major Rivers	Guoyas, Esmeraldos, Blanco, Río Quijos Napo
Mountains	Andes Mountain Range, Cordilleras
Highest Point	Chimborazo, 20,000 feet (6,310 meters)
Official Language	Spanish

Other Languages	Quichua (language of Incas), Shuar (Amazon)
Ethnic Groups	Quichua (Indians), 50 percent; Mestizos, 40 percent; American Indians, 1.5 percent; white, 8.5 percent
Religions	Roman Catholic, 93 percent
Literacy Rate	90 percent
Average Life Expectancy	70 years

Economy

Natural Resources	Oil, fish, gold
Division of Labor Force	Farming, 33 percent; manufacturing, 11 percent
Agricultural Products	Bananas, coffee, and flowers
Major Exports	Oil, fish, bananas, coffee, cocao
Currency	Sucre

Government

Form of Government	Republic
Government Bodies	Chamber of Representatives
Formal Head of State	President
Other Chief Officials	Vice President
Voting Rights	All citizens over the age of 18

HISTORY AT A GLANCE

800-1532   Extensive city-states appear during the Integration period, with small pyramids and other advanced architecture.

1500s   Incas replace local tribes as the dominant group in the region. Quito becomes the northern capital of the Inca empire, with a road linking it to Cuzco.

1532   Quito is destroyed by the Incas to keep it from falling into the hands of the Spanish.

1534   Spanish Quito is founded on the ruins of the Inca city using stone from the original city for building. Franciscans found a school in Quito to teach European painting and sculpture to Indians.

1535   Galapagos Islands accidentally discovered by the Bishop of Panama during a storm. They become a haven for pirates.

1539   Francisco Pizarro makes his brother Gonzalo governor of Quito.

1542   An expedition under Gonzalo Pizarro leaves Quito in search of gold. A part of the expedition reaches the Amazon and sails all the way to the

Atlantic coast. They are the first Europeans to navigate the entire length of the Amazon.

1553   Flemish Franciscan Jodoco Ricke introduces wheat to Ecuador. He also begins the church of San Francisco in Quito, said to be the first Spanish church in South America.

1743   French expedition under La Condamine embarks on raft expedition down Amazon, the first scientific examination of the area. La Condamine's map of the area remains a standard for over a century.

1809   Revolt against Spanish rule in Quito. Spanish restore order after three months.

1810-1812   Further unsuccessful revolts against Spanish rule.

1819   Ecuador declared by Bolívar and other leaders to be part of new independent nation of Gran Colombia, along with New Granada (Colombia) and Venezuela. Spanish nonetheless remain in control in Ecuador.

1821   Having liberated Colombia and Venezuela, Bolívar turns his attention to Ecuador. His general Antonio de Sucre helps local patriots liberate Guayaquil, although Quito remains in Spanish hands. San Martin also sends troops from Chile and Argentina to aid Guayaquil.

1822   Bolívar arrives and defeats the Spanish at Bombona (April 7). The liberation of Ecuador is assured.

1830   Gran Colombia breaks up, with New Granada, Venezuela and Ecuador becoming separate nations.

1832	Ecuador formally lays claim to Galapagos Islands.
1835	Charles Darwin visits Galapagos on board HMS *Beagle*. His description of the islands in *Origin of Species* in 1859 brings them international fame.
1851-1856	The military regime of Jose Maria Urbina, which abolishes slavery (1853).
1860-1875	The dictatorship of Gabriel Garcia Moreno. He attempts to increase religious influence in the country, especially promoting the cult of the Sacred Heart.
1895-1911	The coastal elite comes to power under Eloy Alfaro. Although dictatorial, this regime attempts to modernize the country with numerous reforms.
1925-1931	The Quito elite re-asserts control through a military government.
1942	Boundary dispute with Peru leads to war. The United States mediates a treaty in Rio de Janeiro which cedes most of the disputed land to Peru.
1948	The economy revives, mainly due to the great increase in banana exports.
1960s	Military seizes power 1963-1966, but conservative landowners force return to civilian rule.
1970s	Development of oil production in Oriente province benefits economy, until decline of prices in the late 80s.
1972-1979	Military regime attempts to use oil revenues to modernize country.
1979	Lasting democratic government restored.

1987 Major earthquake damages oil pipeline and many historic buildings.

1990s Increase in environmental legislation and creation of new national parks and wildlife preserves. Tourism increases, especially to the Galapagos Islands.

1995 Military clashes with Peru over longstanding boundary dispute.

1

The Country and the People

Ecuador takes its name from the equator, which crosses the mountains just north of Quito, the capital city. Sandwiched between Colombia and Peru, Ecuador is one of the smallest nations in South America. But it has an extraordinary variety of climates and landscapes, from tropical rainforests to windswept snow peaks. The Galápagos Islands, about 620 miles (1,000 kilometers) west of the Pacific coast, are also part of Ecuador.

The Andes form a huge mountain chain down the middle of the country. Ecuadoreans call the highlands the *Sierra*, and the coastal lowlands the *Costa*. East of the Andes stretches the forested Amazon region, known as the *Oriente*. Altogether, Ecuador covers about 110,000 square miles (284,000 square kilometers), making it larger than the United Kingdom and smaller than Italy. The population has grown fast in recent years and is now over eleven million.

Both the highlands and the lowlands had been inhabited for several thousand years when the Spaniards arrived in South

America. The Incas, a powerful tribe in southern Peru, had built an empire which stretched along the Andes beyond Quito. There were many other tribes in the area too. The Spaniards called them all "Indians," because Christopher Columbus thought he had reached India when he landed in the Americas. He was sailing westward, hoping to find a new trade route from Europe to Asia. It was soon after his discoveries that Spanish expeditions set out to explore and conquer the newly-discovered lands.

The rural population of the highlands and the Amazon region is a mix of Indian and *mestizos*. On the coast and in the cities there are more *mestizos*. *Mestizos* are the result of generations of intermarriage between Indians and Europeans. Apart from Indians, *mestizos* and Europeans, Ecuador also has a black population descended from Africans brought to the country as slaves.

Throughout Ecuador's history the massive Andes mountain have

Mestizo **children in Guayaquil on Ecuador's coast.**

A village in the highlands of Ecuador.

hampered trade and communications between the *Costa*, the *Sierra* and the *Oriente*. The deep ravines and dense wet forests on the flanks of the mountains exhausted the energy of early travellers. Even today, heavy rains and landslides often wash away sections of the roads and railways which connect the coast and the highlands. It is much easier to travel along the broad Andean valleys, or on the lowland plains.

Two majestic mountain ranges–the eastern and western *Cordilleras*–form rims either side of the upland valleys. The Andes are about 75 miles (120 kilometers) wide as they sweep through Ecuador. (They run the full length of South America, from Venezuela to Chile.) Snow-capped peaks rise from the Cordilleras, towering above the central valleys. The highest mountain is Chimborazo at over 20,000 feet (6,310 meters), and there are seven others which are over 16,400 feet (5,000 meters).

Many of the peaceful-looking peaks disguise active volcanoes—so much so that an English explorer called this "The Avenue of the Volcanoes." Cotopaxi, a near-perfect snow-covered cone and the highest active volcano in the world at 19,346 feet (5,897 meters), has a particularly violent history. In the mid-nineteenth century there were several major eruptions and part of Cotopaxi's ice-cap melted. Enormous mud avalanches are said to have buried galloping horsemen, and reached as far as Esmeraldas, on the coast. Volcanoes are not the only threat in the Andes. The cities of Quito, Ambato, Riobamba and Ibarra have all been partly destroyed by earthquakes, and tremors are common.

Cotopaxi, in the eastern *Cordillera*. At 19,345 feet (5,897 meters), this is the highest active volcano in the world.

Between the *Cordilleras* lies a series of densely populated fertile basins. Their average altitude is about 8,200 feet (2,500 meters), with a pleasant, mild climate. Most of the rain falls between November and May—the wet season is in winter, and the dry season summer. Temperatures vary more within twenty-four hours than they do through the year, because of the influence of the equator. There is a difference of only 5.4 degrees Fahrenheit (3 degrees Celsius) between the average for the hottest month (60.8 degrees Fahrenheit–16 degrees Celsius) and the coldest month (55.4 degrees Fahrenheit–13 degrees Celsius).

The highland basins shelter Quito (with over one million people), as well as several medium-sized cities. Many crops, including maize, wheat, apples, avocados and vegetables are produced on the volcanic soils. Higher up the slopes of the *Cordilleras* the climate is

Growing maize near Cañar in the highlands.

harsher, with strong winds, hail-storms and night frosts. Here there are scattered villages and hardier crops such as barley, potatoes and local Andean roots and grains. Few people live above 13,123 feet (4,000 meters), where little grows and sheep graze on the cold grasslands called *páramo*.

Rivers cut steep gorges through the eastern and western *Cordilleras*. Those flowing east eventually join the Atlantic Ocean, and those going west feed the Pacific. As they reach the coastal lowlands, the rivers broaden and deposit silt on the flood-plains. This makes excellent farmland where all kinds of tropical crops can be planted.

About half of Ecuador's population lives in the coastal region. Guayaquil, the chief sea port, industrial and commercial center is larger than Quito. It has over 1.5 million people, and thousands more flock to the city every year. Guayaquil is hot and muggy in the wet season, between January and May, when temperatures average 80 degrees Fahrenheit (27 degrees Celsius). But it becomes fresher in the dry season, and the temperature falls by 3 or 4 degrees.

In the northern part of the *Costa* the rains are heaviest, and the forested landscape is lush green all the year round. Moving southward the wet season becomes shorter until, near the border with Peru, there is only brownish, scrubby vegetation as a result of the lack of rain. The driest area of Ecuador is the Santa Elena peninsula, west of Guayaquil. In some years there is no rain at all there. The desert is spreading because, in order to obtain firewood, people cut down the few bushes that can still grow.

Ecuador has about 620 miles (1,000 kilometers) of coastline, with long sandy beaches, rocky headlands and mangrove swamps. Five

One of Ecuador's fine sandy beaches near Esmeraldas.

thousand years ago there were already fishing communities along the shore. Although they have more sophisticated nets nowadays, the fishermen still bring their catch through the surf onto the village beaches. The cool ocean current flowing northward from Peru (the Humboldt Current) has rich stocks of fish. Bigger boats go out for these shoals from Manta, Esmeraldas and other fishing-ports.

Far out in the Pacific, also on the equator, are the Galápagos Islands; there are six main islands and dozens of smaller ones. About ten thousand people live on them. Giant tortoises, called *galápagos* in Spanish, gave the islands their name. Many of the plants and animals there are unique. It was on these islands that Charles Darwin saw some of the species that led to his theory of evolution. The islands are protected by the government, and tourism is

20

controlled to preserve the environment.

The Amazon region still has a small population, although it is growing fast. Since 1972, when Amazon oil production began, the region has become much more important. Settlers from the highlands—called colonists—are hacking down the forest to make farms. Near the foothills of the Andes, the land is quite hilly and there is a lot of pasture for cattle. Most of the Amazon Indians live further east where the rivers are used as highways, and the jungle provides good hunting.

With so many different environments, Ecuador also has a wide range of plants and animals. On the most isolated parts of the high *páramo,* deer and condors still survive. The condor is an enormous vulture—its wings may measure more than nearly ten feet (three meters) across. The *páramo* plants include blue, purple, red and yellow gentians, and the strange, spiky, *frailejon* that sticks up above the clumps of long grass. Trees only grow at this altitude if they are well-sheltered; but tough bushes with multicolored flowers resist the strong winds.

There are more than three thousand kinds of orchids in Ecuador, growing from sea level up to the cold *páramo.* Bright red and yellow orchids cling to lowland trees, while delicate pink and purple varieties flourish in the mountains. Over 130 different species of hummingbirds have been recorded. These dazzling little birds have beaks shaped to fit the kinds of flowers they feed on. Ecuador is also known for its large number of beautiful butterflies, especially the iridescent blue morphos.

The jungle is full of extraordinary plants. The giant trees that form the forest canopy hide hundreds of creepers, ferns, fungi, fruit trees and flowering shrubs. Mahogany, cinnamon, rubber and curare (a poison which paralyses the muscles) are all jungle products. Although there is no shortage of insects, frogs and brilliant birds, the larger animals are disappearing. People hunt jaguars, alligators and anacondas to sell their skins. As more of the forest is cut down, monkeys, anteaters and tapirs are becoming scarcer too.

The Spaniards were impressed by the variety of landscapes and civilizations they found in South America. But, above all, they were impressed by the quantity of gold they saw in Inca palaces. This led them to call their newly conquered territory "El Dorado"–the Golden Land. The Kingdom of Quito (roughly equivalent to modern Ecuador) produced less gold than other Spanish colonies. Instead, it had rich farmland and a large Indian population that could be forced to serve the conquerors.

After it gained independence from Spain in 1822, Ecuador became a republic. The president, vice-president and congressional representatives are elected for four years by Ecuadoreans over the age of eighteen. There are national and provincial congressmen belonging to several political parties. The country is divided into twenty-one provinces, and each province elects its own local government and councillors. However, several times in Ecuador's history military or civilian dictators have taken control and ruled without holding elections.

Spanish is the official language of Ecuador, but most highland Indians still speak Quichua, the Inca language. Other languages are spoken by Indian groups in the Amazon and coastal regions.

Although schools teach in Spanish, there are many bilingual education programs which keep the old languages alive. A few radio stations even broadcast in Quichua and in Shuar, an Amazon language.

As a result of recent efforts to teach people to read and write, only ten percent of the adult population is illiterate. But about half of the children who start primary school never complete the course. In the countryside many of them have to help their families by looking after the animals or doing household chores. The Catholic Church founded the first schools in Ecuador, and the Church still runs some teaching and training programs. Most Ecuadoreans are Catholics, though Protestant and other missionaries also work in Ecuador.

Just over half the country's population lives in towns and cities. On the whole, people in urban areas have a higher standard of living than people in the countryside. That is, more houses have electricity, water and sewage services, more children go to school, and more families have television sets. But there are big gaps between the few who live in large brick houses with gardens, and the many who make their homes in wooden shacks on wasteland.

In the countryside, too, the difference between the rich and the poor is much greater than it is in developed countries. Most of the land is owned by a few people. Peasant families often find it impossible to produce enough on their small plots of land to feed themselves. Some members of the family may have to go to the city to try and get a job. Although Ecuador has the highest population density in South America—about 95 people per square mile (42 people per square kilometer)—there is still a lot of land that could be farmed.

More than three million Ecuadoreans are employed, and the majority work on the land or in service jobs. It is often difficult to find a full-time job, with proper wages and social security benefits. So people have to think up ways to earn money, such as washing clothes, running errands or cleaning car windscreens.

Until 1972, Ecuador's development was based almost entirely on agricultural products. Then oil exports brought in more foreign earnings, and new manufacturing industries began to provide more jobs in the cities. About twelve percent of all the people employed work in industry, especially food and textile factories. Some electrical goods and chemical products are also made locally, but

A glittering-bellied emerald hummingbird.

Many types of frog, such as this brightly-colored tree frog, inhabit the Ecuadorean jungle.

most modern machinery has to be imported. For example, turbines for power stations and communications equipment must be bought from other countries.

Both Quito and Guayaquil have international airports, and national airlines fly to the Galápagos Islands and to most cities. But distances in Ecuador are not too great, and road travel is more common. The Pan-American Highway, which connects all the Andean countries, is paved from the northern frontier with Colombia as far as the Peruvian border, south of Guayaquil. The paved highway system has developed rapidly and bus travel has improved greatly since modernization in 1994. Two railway

25

Boarding an Ecuatoriana Airlines plane at Quito airport.

lines—one from Quito to Guayaquil, and one from Ibarra to San Lorenzo on the northwest coast—also link the *Sierra* and the *Costa* but railway service is often very unreliable due to varying weather conditions.

2

Incas and Spaniards

Ecuador's first inhabitants probably arrived from the north over twelve thousand years ago. They would have been descendants of people who crossed from Asia to North America when the northern parts of these continents were connected by a land bridge. Others may have come across the Pacific Ocean to the coast of South America. They were mainly hunters who also gathered plants and lived in small groups. By 3000 B.C. some of these people were already growing their own food and settling into more permanent homes.

Unfortunately many of Ecuador's pre-Spanish settlements have been torn apart by greedy treasure-hunters digging for gold and ancient pottery. Even so, archaeologists have found a great many clay figures, decorated pots, mother-of-pearl fishing hooks and other objects which allow them to piece together a picture of some periods of the past.

Early lowland farmers grew maize, sweet potatoes, peanuts, peppers and cotton. Some of these products were traded with the highlanders, who planted potatoes and other root crops, and kept llamas for their wool. Gold jewelry and copper tools became more common as metalworking techniques improved. Although travel was slow and difficult, trade routes were established across the Andes to the Amazon, and to the far north and south. As the population grew and agriculture became more efficient, imposing temples and towns were built.

At the beginning of the fifteenth century there were many different chiefdoms in what is now Ecuador. The chief usually lived in a town, together with his warriors, priests and craftsmen. Farmers brought their products to market in the towns and joined in the religious festivals there. More often than not, neighboring chiefdoms

A pottery figure, dating from the period between 500 B.C. and A.D. 500, now exhibited in Quito's Central Bank museum.

The Ingapirca fortress in Cañar.

would be at war with each other, but occasionally alliances were made. When the Incas began to extend their empire northward from Peru, they had great difficulty defeating tribal alliances in the Cañar and Otavalo regions. North of Otavalo, a lake was stained red with the blood of all the warriors massacred by the Inca troops. Since then it has been called Yawarcocha, which means "lake of blood" in Quichua.

Led by Huayna Capac, the Incas eventually conquered all of highland Ecuador. They built stone palaces, temples and forts. Relay runners sped along the road that linked Quito with Cuzco, the Inca capital. They took only eight days to carry messages nearly 1,200 miles (2,000 kilometers) through the Andes. Inca officials reorganized the highland tribes and introduced the Quichua

29

language, which is still widely spoken. Only a few Inca ruins remain today. The royal palaces at Tomebamba (modern Cuenca) were destroyed, but much of the fine Ingapirca fortress and sun temple still stands in Cañar.

Although the Incas ruled in Ecuador for only a short time, they made every effort to impose their customs and religion. Part of each year's harvest had to be handed over to the authorities, and people had to worship the Inca emperor and his god, the sun. If a newly conquered community seemed rebellious, the emperor might order people to be moved away to another part of the empire. If he needed warriors for his armies, he took them from the villages. In exchange for obedience and hard work, everyone was given food and was cared for by the state.

In 1527, when Huayna Capac was in Quito, he learned that bearded white strangers had been seen on the coast. He died soon after, probably of smallpox brought by the foreigners. Two of Huayna Capac's sons—Atahualpa and Huascar—were soon fighting for control of the Inca empire. Atahualpa, who was based in Quito, marched southward and his generals captured Huascar. Then there was news from the lowlands of more strange white men.

This time it was Francisco Pizarro at the head of a small but determined Spanish army. When Atahualpa heard there were fewer than two hundred soldiers, he allowed the Spaniards to cross the Andes mountains and meet him in the city of Cajamarca, in northern Peru. But Atahualpa's huge and splendid army had primitive means of transport and weapons compared with the Spaniards' horses, cannon and armor.

A painting which depicts the first landing in South America of the Spanish conquistador, Francisco Pizarro in the early sixteenth century.

Pizarro launched a surprise attack in Cajamarca's main square, and more than seven thousand Indians were slaughtered in two hours. Atahualpa was taken prisoner. He offered to fill a room with gold, in exchange for his freedom. But once the gold had been fetched from all over the Inca empire, the Spaniards broke the agreement and executed Atahualpa.

Quito proved a more difficult prize. Rumiñahui (one of Atahualpa's generals) fought battle after battle against the Spanish troops as they advanced up the Andes. Yet at last Rumiñahui was forced to flee Quito. And when the Spaniards arrived they found empty, burnt-out ruins instead of the fabulous treasure they had hoped for.

The conquerors *(conquistadores* in Spanish) established in Quito in

31

1534 and Guayaquil in 1535. At first they fought among themselves, but the Spanish king sent out a representative to restore order. Administrators arrived from Spain to organize the new colony, which was known as the *Real Audiencia de Quito* (Royal Audience of Quito). A *Real Audiencia* was a court of justice; and in this case the term was used for the area under the court's jurisdiction. It extended farther north and east than Ecuador does today, and at first it came under the rule of the Spanish viceroy in Lima (Peru). Although there were local law courts and city councils, most of the laws were made in Spain.

At the time of the conquest there were probably more than half a million Indians living in the *Real Audiencia de Quito*. Wars and diseases brought from abroad killed so many that by the end of the sixteenth century only 200,000 Indians were left. From the beginning the American Indians were treated by the conquerors as inferiors. In theory, laws protected them from slavery and allowed them to keep their land. But the *conquistadores* were "awarded" a certain number of Indians on condition that they converted the Indians to Roman Catholicism and looked after them. The Indians had to pay tithes and taxes and give their labor to their new masters. The Spaniards gradually seized all the best lands, especially the fertile highland valleys. Although the Indians rebelled on many occasions, they were unable to change the appalling conditions in which they lived.

Religious orders were founded in Quito, and enormous sums were spent on building splendid churches and monasteries. The Church started schools in the cities, but they were mainly for

Spanish children. Missionaries went off on hair-raising journeys to the Amazon and the coast to teach Christianity to the Indians.

The Spaniards introduced sheep, cattle and new crops, such as wheat, to their new colonies. On the big estates—called *haciendas*—they set up textile workshops to make cheap cloth. At first Guayaquil was a shipbuilding center for the whole Pacific coast; then tobacco, sugarcane and cocoa were planted on the lowlands.

Towards the end of the eighteenth century the locally-born Spaniards and *mestizos* grew impatient with the laws and officials imposed by Spain. They wanted greater freedom to trade with other countries, to choose their own authorities and to decide what taxes they should pay. The first blow for independence was struck in the city of Quito. On August 10, 1809, a revolutionary government was proclaimed and crowds poured out onto the streets to celebrate.

Although the first Quito government lasted for less than three months, and thirty-six revolutionaries were brutally murdered, the colonies were soon to be free. After Guayaquil declared independence in 1820, fighting broke out in many parts of the country. The war between the pro-Spanish forces and the rebels had already spread all over the South American continent. Spaniards, *mestizos* and Indians fought in the armies, and even British soldiers went to join the rebels.

The northern liberation armies were commanded by Simón Bolívar, a brilliant Venezuelan soldier with a driving determination to win freedom from Spain. As Bolívar led his troops to victory in Colombia and Venezuela, one of his generals fought a decisive battle above Quito.

This statue of Simón Bolívar, one of the leading figures in South America's struggle to win independence from Spain, stands outside the cathedral in Guayaquil.

Antonio José de Sucré and three thousand soldiers climbed the steep slopes of Pichincha in darkness. On the morning of May 24, 1822 they were hiding in the gulleys overlooking Quito. Royalist Spanish batallions marched up from the city but, after three hours of fierce fighting, they were forced back down the mountain. The president of the *Real Audiencia de Quito* surrendered and Sucre entered the city triumphantly. Many years later, Ecuador's coin, the sucre, was named in his honor.

3

The Republic

The victory on the mountain slopes above Quito won independence for Ecuador. After the long struggle against Spain, there was great political confusion in the Andean countries. At first Colombia, Ecuador and Venezuela joined together in one nation as the liberator Simón Bolívar had hoped. In 1830, however, they separated. Ecuador's first constitution was drawn up, and Juan José Flores, one of Simón Bolívar's generals, became president.

In the 160 years following independence Ecuador had eighteen constitutions and more than eighty-five governments. From the beginning there were military revolts, Indian rebellions, civilian uprisings, and dictatorships. Many of the presidents took power by force rather than being elected by the people, although Ecuador was officially a democratic republic.

Quito, the highland capital, and Guayaquil, the Pacific port, competed for political and economic power. Guayaquil's wealth came from tropical crops grown on the lowlands. For a time it was the world's leading cocoa exporter, supplying chocolate manufacturers in Europe and North America. By the end of the nineteenth century iron foundries and food industries were flourishing in Guayaquil and it had become a busy financial center too.

The journey from Guayaquil to Quito was difficult and dangerous, especially in the rainy season. Travellers had to take canoes up the river to Babahoyo, then ride mules up steep rocky paths through the dripping forest. Fast-flowing rivers had to be crossed on flimsy bridges made of rope and wood. The ice-cold mountain passes were often hidden in the mist.

Construction of the railway joining Guayaquil and Quito was begun by Gabriel García Moreno, who ruled Ecuador from 1860. He was a severe, religious man, determined to impose order and progress even if it meant being a tyrant. Apart from developing agriculture and industry, he also helped create a feeling of national identity. There were fewer political upheavals during this period but, in 1875, García Moreno was assassinated as he walked across the square from Quito's cathedral to the presidential palace.

The railway project was revived by General Eloy Alfaro, Guayaquil's great revolutionary hero. He fought the ruling Conservatives for many years, and defeated them with a rebel Liberal army in 1895. The people believed he stood for freedom and justice, and that he would protect the poor and the Indians. Once he became president, Eloy Alfaro improved education and health services and limited the power of the Catholic Church. Small and energetic, he transformed backward Quito by installing electric light, trams and sewage systems.

This steam-powered locomotive, dating from 1901, runs on the Quito-Guayaquil line. The line was begun by Gabriel García Moreno, who ruled Ecuador from 1860 to 1875 when he was assassinated.

The railway was a tremendous venture; whole mountainsides had to be dynamited for the steep Devil's Nose (*Nariz del Diablo*) section. Torrential rains and huge landslides tore away parts of the track. But, at last, in 1908 the first train reached Quito. After all his efforts to change conditions in Ecuador, Eloy Alfaro met the same fate as Gabriel García Moreno. He too was murdered.

From 1900 on, new lowland crops such as coffee and rice were exported, and oil was discovered in the Santa Elena peninsula. But Ecuador's cocoa earnings, which had brought great wealth to Guayaquil, began to decline, food prices went soaring up, and people poured out onto the streets to protest. In 1922 the Guayaquil trade unions called a general strike that finished in tragedy—more

37

than one thousand people were killed.

After independence, Ecuador had to defend its borders on many occasions. Even so, chunks of territory were cut away by neighboring countries. In 1941 Peruvian troops advanced into southern Ecuador, occupying parts of the coast, the highlands and the Amazon region. The following year the Ecuadorean government had to agree to sign the Rio de Janeiro Treaty, which gave Peru much of Ecuador's Amazon territory. As one section of the southeastern border was not properly defined, skirmishes continued long afterwards. According to Ecuador, the treaty is still not acceptable, nor can it be put into effect, so the area remains in dispute.

Ecuador's political turmoils have been compared with the volcanic eruptions and earthquakes that often shake the country. One of the most unpredictable rulers was José María Velasco Ibarra, who first became president in 1934. A persuasive orator, Velasco Ibarra said that as long as he had a balcony to speak from, the people would vote for him. He was elected five times and only once lasted out the full presidential term. During his fifth term of government, he abolished congress and made himself dictator. But soon after this the army took power from him.

The armed forces governed from 1972 to 1979. This was a time of important social and economic changes. New oilfields in the Amazon region brought sudden wealth to the country, construction and modern industries blossomed in Quito and Guayaquil; and there was money to spend on building roads, schools and shopping centers. The government encouraged colonists to start new farms in the lowlands and began a land reform program in the highlands. This freed the Indians who were still working in near-slavery as *huasipungos* on the Andean estates. *Huasipungo* means "door of the house" in Quichua, and the *huasipungo* was an Indian who had to stay close to the master's door and serve him. Once he owned his piece of land, the Indian was free to make his own choices.

At the end of the military dictatorship elections were held–first to vote on a new constitution, then to choose a civilian president. There was great political activity, with new political parties being formed and excitement about the return to democracy. Congressional representatives were elected once again, and politicians made generous promises. The old rivalry between Quito and Guayaquil, still strong, sharpened debates in congress. Jaime Roldós Aguilera was elected president in 1979, after a long and lively campaign. Less than two years after becoming president he was killed in a plane crash and the vice-president, Osvaldo Hurtado Larrea, replaced him.

Ecuadoreans expected democratic government to make life easier and to raise family incomes. When things hardly changed, there were strikes and street demonstrations. The elected presidents have found it difficult to persuade congress to approve new laws proposed by the government. There are no large political parties in Ecuador, so each president has had to form a shaky alliance of several groups to support him in congress.

As Ecuador returned to civilian rule, the economic situation was becoming much worse in all Latin America. This meant less money to spend on hospitals and housing. For ordinary Ecuadoreans, life

Voting in a small town in the Ecuadorean highlands.

became more expensive and jobs were more difficult to find. Recent governments have tried to improve living conditions in the countryside, but many children still go without medical care and secondary schooling. The population of cities such as Guayaquil is growing too fast for water and other services to keep pace. But people often work together to find their own ways of solving these problems, just as they did long before the Spaniards arrived.

4

Ancient and Modern Quito

Nestling in the Andes, Quito has a spectacular setting. Its past has been punctuated by natural disasters and political dramas. In about 500 B.C. a thriving settlement at the base of Pichincha was devastated by lava and ash. The site was rediscovered when bulldozers started cutting roads for a new housing estate near the airport. They churned up so many broken pots and bones that archaeologists began to investigate. Underneath the volcanic pumice they found the remains of houses, as well as obsidian knives (made from vitreous lava), polished stone bowls and decorated pottery. The village had apparently been there for more than 1,500 years before it was buried.

The Incas made Quito an important military base and the main government center for the northern part of the empire. It was Atahualpa's home, and the Spaniards wrote accounts of fine stone buildings, storehouses and fortifications. But these were destroyed before the Spanish *conquistadores* took possession of the city. Today, the nearest Inca monument is a hilltop fortress at Rumicucho, where religious ceremonies were also held. Rumicucho guarded the approach to Quito against attacks by the fierce northern tribes.

The Spaniards founded San Francisco de Quito (the original full name of the capital) in 1534. Soon afterwards the main squares or *plazas* were laid out. The hub of the city has always been the *Plaza de Independencia* (Independence Square), dominated by the presidential palace. The cathedral, the city offices and the archbishop's palace, which has been renovated into shops, complete the other three sides of the square. Although the plaza has seen assassinations, coups and riots, it also makes a peaceful place for people to sit and read newspapers while they have their shoes polished.

San Francisco is a magnificent plaza, always full of activity. Street

The presidential palace which dominates the magnificent Plaza de Independencia (Independence Square), Quito.

sellers offer chunks of pineapple or popcorn. Indians bent double under enormous loads head for the markets. Atahualpa's father, the Inca Huayna Capac, is said to have built a great palace here. Now the San Francisco church and monastery, begun in the sixteenth century, overlook the square. The original church towers were destroyed in one of Quito's earthquakes, and were replaced by much smaller ones. Intricate carvings, beautiful sculptures and paintings fill the inside of the church, which glows with light reflected from the gold leaf covering the altars. People often stop by the main door to buy a candle to burn in front of their favorite religious image.

The religious orders competed in building sumptuous churches. Indians provided the labor, and local craftsmen became extraordinarily skilled. Gold was brought from mines far north and south of Quito to gild the interiors. The city was known throughout the continent for its sculptors, painters and woodcarvers. Their work can be seen in monasteries and churches such as Santo Domingo, San Diego, La Compania and La Merced. Miguel de Santiago was one of the most famous painters in Quito. His series showing the life of Saint Augustine lines the cloisters of the San Augustin monastery.

Much of the colonial center of Quito has been preserved. The steep narrow streets are lined with old buildings painted white and blue. Balconies overhang the pavements, and great stone gateways now lead into offices, shops and overcrowded homes. The house in which Sucré lived is built round an open courtyard or *patio,* like many other colonial residences.

Buses and cars jam the streets in the center of Quito. But a

A scene from the life of Saint Augustine, painted by Miguel de Santiago, in the cloisters of the San Augustin monastery in Quito.

highway with long tunnels runs along the side of Pichincha, bypassing the busiest areas.

The equator crosses the Andes 14 miles (23 kilometers) north of Quito. A monument marks the spot where it is possible to stand with one foot in the northern hemisphere and one in the southern hemisphere. In 1735 a French expedition led by Charles de la Condamine came to measure the exact position of the equatorial line. The scientists spent so many years trying to take accurate readings that the authorities of Quito became suspicious. They thought the expedition must be looking for gold.

What was once a small city tucked unobtrusively into the folds of Pichincha has spread far north and south. It has also spilled over the eastern hills into the broad valley below. Just under one of the ridges lined with skyscrapers is the church of Guápulo, which has a beautifully carved pulpit; and fine paintings. New houses are now eating into the farmland in the lower valley, where the climate is warmer and where orchards and vegetable gardens dot the landscape.

The *Panecillo* (a hill shaped like a bread roll) looms over the colonial center. Before the Spaniards arrived, the sun was

A street in the old colonial center of Quito. The hill in the background is the *Panecillo*, surmounted by a huge statue of the Virgin Mary.

worshipped here. Now a statue of the Virgin Mary stands on top of the hill. Long avenues such as the Sixth of December (the anniversary of Quito's foundation) and the Tenth of August (the day independence was declared) stretch northward towards the airport. One of the busiest shopping streets is Amazonas, lined with banks, restaurants and craft shops. Tall skyscrapers housing offices and homes rise up among the older buildings.

Green mountain slopes are gradually being taken over by residential areas, which also reach north towards the equator. On Sundays the parks are packed with people playing soccer or basketball, and families picnicking on the grass.

Street stalls and open-air markets used to abound throughout the city but were officially abolished in 1981. Street markets still take place though on a few streets throughout the city and vendors still offer the beautiful produce and handicrafts of the countryside.

So many poor people have moved to the capital that it is difficult for them to find places to live. Some families squeeze together in small rooms in the old colonial houses. The fountain in the patio may be the only place to wash. Others collect building materials and knock together homes on unoccupied land. They hope the city authorities will eventually put in roads and waterpipes. A few manage to buy cheap flats or houses constructed by the government.

For a long time Quito was fairly isolated, high up in the mountains. Although it was always the main government center, industry was slow to develop there. Today it is on the Pan American Highway, and roads lead west to the Pacific coast and east to the Amazon region. Industrial plants making cars, clothing, food products and chemicals have grown up along the main routes out of the city. It is also the cultural focus for Ecuador; painters of today exhibit their work in modern art galleries not far from the museums which house colonial treasures, and ceramics made thousands of years ago.

5

Life in the Highlands

It is often possible to tell which village a highlander comes from by looking at his poncho. People living in towns no longer use ponchos very much, but out in the countryside they give excellent protection from the cold and rain. In the Otavalo area, men wear dark blue ponchos over white cotton trousers. Around Latacunga, a strong red weave is common, and farther south the Saraguro Indians dress almost entirely in black.

Indians wearing their distinctive, heavy woollen ponchos.

A small Indian community high in the mountains.

Highland Indian women wear embroidered blouses with long skirts and brightly-colored belts wound round and round the waist. Instead of a poncho, they have a thick woollen cloth or shawl knotted over the shoulders. Another square of cloth is used for carrying a baby on the back, or for taking the maize cobs home from the fields. Apart from looking after their children, feeding the animals, spinning wool and collecting firewood, the women also do some of the sowing and harvesting.

Rural life in the *Sierra* depends largely on the altitude and the seasons. The climate changes suddenly from one mountainside to another according to whether there is plenty of rain or not. Parts of the Andes are very dry, and the stony slopes covered with cactus and tough bushes are only fit for goats. On the highest *páramos*, the

49

ice-cold lakes have trout in them, but no crops can be grown. In the far south, the mountains are lower and the climate is more mild.

Many Indian communities are hidden in the *Cordilleras,* far above the temperate Andean valleys. Fruit plantations and dairy farms occupy the best land along the broad valley floors, while the Indians have small plots on the mountain slopes. After centuries of cultivation, the fields are worn away. When heavy rain falls, the soil may be washed off and sandy patches exposed.

Until recently, highland Indians usually worked on the big estates or *haciendas* in exchange for a piece of land. Now some work for wages, and others farm their own plots. Co-operatives have been started up, and the Indians join together to buy seeds or a truck to take their products to market. The government often supports the co-operatives, using loans from international organizations. Villagers may share the highest land, where everyone's sheep and

Llamas on Mount Cotopaxi.

cattle can graze. Children take the animals up to the pastures in the morning, and bring them down in the evening. In some of the *páramo* communities, llama herds are kept for their wool.

Indian families are generally big, and with each new generation there are more mouths to feed from the same plot of land. While the older people continue planting crops, the young leave home. They may go to the cities to study and look for a job, or to work on the coastal sugarcane plantations for a few months every year. Highlanders always like to be at home in June, to help with the harvest and enjoy the festivals.

Older-style houses in the countryside are made of mud bricks and wood, with thatch or tiles on the roof. There is not much space or light inside the house, so people often sit outside to do household jobs. Children may help to peel potatoes or prepare wool for spinning. The weaving loom is set up in a sheltered spot—some ancient back-strap looms, similar to those used in pre-Inca days, are still in use. Apart from making their own clothes and blankets, highland Indians also weave patterned belts and striped ponchos to sell to tourists.

The Otavalo region is famous for all kinds of woolen goods including wall hangings, sweaters, jackets and scarves. Each village has its own specialties, and some products are exported to other countries. Every Saturday Otavalo Indians put their work on show in the Poncho Plaza, and the market is a big attraction for tourists. Early in the day, the local people trade in sheep's wool and dyes of all colors, as well as bright threads for embroidering blouses.

Since pre-Spanish times highlanders have worked together on

51

Highland villagers at work on a *minga* (community project).

community projects, called *mingas*. Sometimes a particular day—for instance, every other Monday—is set aside to keep irrigation ditches and roads in good order. Communities may be given the materials to build a school, provided the villagers do all the work; or a family building a new house will invite the neighbors to help, in exchange for lots of food and maize beer or *chicha*.

Few families in the countryside have electricity and running water. Clothes are usually washed in mountain lakes and streams. Every day someone has to fetch water from the nearest village tap or stream for cooking. This makes it difficult to keep food clean, and small children often have stomach illnesses. Vaccination campaigns and new health posts benefit some villages. But many people still rely on traditional healers who use herbs and a little magic. There are herb experts in the markets, offering advice and bundles of camomile or spearmint leaves.

Nearly every highland town has a weekly market which brings people flocking in from the countryside. Laden Indians set off from their villages on foot, in buses and in trucks while it is still dark. Carrying potatoes, onions, chickens, cheeses, earthenware pots and crafts, they arrive early to sell their produce. Much of the bargaining is done in *Quichua*. The Saquisili Thursday market is one of the most popular. It spills over into every plaza and alleyway of the small town. Long ropes made of fiber from the spiky cabuya plant are coiled in one area; huge piles of reed mats and baskets occupy

Ropes, made from the fiber of the cabuya plant, on sale in the bustling and colorful market held every Thursday in Saquisilí.

another; sacks full of squeaking animals block the pavements; and everywhere people are jostling to get at the food-stalls.

When Indians leave their villages to live in cities, they usually change their customs and the way they dress. The Otavalo Indians are an exception—even university students continue to wear their distinctive blue and white clothes, while Otavalo men keep their long braided hair.

This is partly because the Otavaleños (as they are called) are recognized as hardworking, go-ahead Indians. Some of them have successful businesses and prosperous farms.

In Ecuador the word *Indio* is sometimes used as an insult. Many young Indians prefer to put aside their ponchos and rope-soled sandals, and buy jeans and sneakers instead. Then they are treated as *mestizos* rather than *Indios*.

The deep Chota valley, which cuts through the northern Andes

An Otavalo Indian man.

from the coastal lowlands, is different from the rest of the *Sierra*. It is much lower (about 4,921 feet −1,500 meters high) and nearly all the people living in the valley are black. The land was once owned by the Jesuits, and they brought back slaves from Colombia and Esmeraldas to work on their sugarcane estates. Slavery was abolished by a government decree in 1851, but most of the blacks went on living on the *haciendas* for many years.

Now some of the black Chota communities have their own land. They grow cotton, fruit and sugarcane on the wet, irrigated valley floor; but much of the area is barren and desert-like. The people in Chota still have some African traditions, and their houses are grouped close together, unlike Indian ones. Alongside the houses are pens for pigs and goats. The women carry large bundles on their heads, and often take their produce into the Ibarra market.

Andean cities, such as Ibarra, Ambato, Riobamba and Loja, are mainly local government and trade centers, with a few small industries. But Cuenca, with more than 200,000 people, is Ecuador's third largest city. It lies in the southern *Sierra*, and a branch line connects it to the Guayaquil-Quito railway. Cuenca still has some cobblestone streets and picturesque colonial houses, though there are hardly any remains of the palaces that the Inca Huayna Capac built.

Cuenca has a long tradition of artists and poets and has been called the "Athens of Ecuador." The city is the focus of a rich farming area with a strong craft tradition. Family businesses produce painted pottery, jewelry, leather goods and embroidered clothes. In nearby Gualaceo, women often sit outside their

Houses of descendants of African slaves, grouped close together, in African style, in the Chota valley of the northern Andes.

houses weaving fine straw hats, known as Panama hats. A great many people in the *Sierra* still rely on old skills to make a living in modern Ecuador.

6

Guayaquil and the Coast

Guayaquil is Ecuador's largest city, as well as the country's main seaport. During its early years, the city was often ravaged by fires and plundered by pirate ships. Although there were forts with powerful cannon on the Santa Ana hills overlooking the river estuary, British and Dutch pirates used to storm ashore to seize provisions and valuables. The houses were made of cane and wood with tiled roofs. They burned only too easily, whether by accident

Old riverboats on the Guayas River.

or when the invaders set fire to them.

The city spread gradually along the waterfront of the Guayas River. Boats of all kinds—canoes, rafts, sailing-ships, and later steamers—were used for transport up the rivers and along the coast. In the rainy season, from January to May, it was practically impossible to travel by land. Goods were taken to the waterside market by boat, and near by there were shipyards for building ocean-going vessels.

A few old houses still survive near the waterfront at the foot of the Santa Ana hills. They lean out at strange angles, and their pretty wooden shutters are usually propped open to let the breeze through. Not so long ago, young girls would sit by the windows to listen to their admirers playing serenades in the street below. At the turn of this century more than 1,800 houses were destroyed in two huge fires. As a result, people began to use more lasting building materials.

Air-conditioned skyscrapers are taking over the main avenue, which is called the Ninth of October in memory of Guayaquil's independence day. In the center, office buildings jut out from the second floor, providing shaded colonnades underneath. It is a noisy, tropical atmosphere, with the occasional snack-bar overflowing onto the pavement.

Along the waterfront passengers board ferries to cross the broad river estuary. Small boats unload cargo, and luxury launches are moored near the yacht club. People buy ice-creams or oysters and sit lazing on park benches under the trees. A statue commemorates the meeting between the two independence heroes, Simón Bolívar and

José de San Martín, who fought to free the northern and southern parts of the continent from Spain.

Guayaquil remained quite small until after independence; but during the nineteenth century more highlanders began to move down to the coastal region. Some worked on the big cocoa and sugarcane plantations in the Guayas river basin, and some went to the city itself. Immigrants arrived from other countries too. Chinese families without entry documents were secretly unloaded inside barrels from cargo ships. Food industries based on lowland crops started up with the help of foreign investors. The city grew steadily more important as a commercial and banking center. By the beginning of this century it was already larger than Quito.

People from the poorer rural areas continue to flood into Guayaquil, looking for a better way of life. The city has spread over mangrove swamps and around tidal inlets. Shaky wooden walkways connect thousands of bamboo shacks built on stilts over the river mud. Bit by bit, the swamps are filled in, roads are bulldozed through, and solid houses replace the shacks. In the more prosperous suburbs, scarlet-flowering acacia trees shade the streets and new shopping centers take shape.

The city extends southward nearly all the way to the new port of Guayaquil. Most of Ecuador's imports are handled by this port, as well as half the exports. On the main roads leading away from Guayaquil there are cigarette factories, prawn-packing plants and cocoa industries, all using raw materials from the coastal region. One of South America's longest bridges spans the Guayas River, carrying traffic eastward.

The fishing port of Manta.

At weekends Guayaquileños drive west through the Santa Elena desert to seaside towns. Salinas is the favorite resort, but there are many villages with sandy beaches along the coast. While Salinas has large hotels, apartment blocks and speed-boats racing along the shore, the villages are quiet fishing-ports on the same sites as some of Ecuador's earliest settlements.

Manta, a little further north, is the biggest fishing-port. Coffee and cotton are grown inland. Panama hats are made in this area, around Montecristi. The fiber for the hats comes from the toquilla plant, which has to be finely shredded. It is important to keep the fiber moist; some people are so careful that they only handle it in the very early morning, when there is dew in the air. Weaving Panama hats is a family tradition. A really first-class one can take more than two

60

months to finish. The best hats, which are usually exported, can be rolled or folded without losing their shape.

The Guayas river basin is fed by dozens of tributaries meandering over the lowlands. In the wet season, floods cover the fields on the low-lying plains, where rice and bananas grow. Cattle are fattened on the lush pastures, and cocoa is produced on the higher land. In some years the rains last longer than usual, causing much more serious flooding. Then crops are damaged, roads disappear and houses are washed away.

Farther south, around Machala, the coastal plain is much narrower. But here too there is rich irrigated soil, and bananas flourish. They are exported from Puerto Bolívar after being washed and packed in cardboard boxes. In fact, bananas seem to grow everywhere on the lowlands. Santo Domingo de los Colorados in the north is another banana region, though it also has big African Palm plantations for producing vegetable oil. Much of this land has only been farmed recently by highland colonists, and the town is growing at a tremendous rate.

Santo Domingo de los Colorados is named after the Colorado Indians who live close by. The Indians have lost most of their land to colonists, and there are very few of them left. The Colorado shamans (medicine-men) were famous for their herb cures and healing rituals. Without enough land to hunt forest animals, the Indians now grow their food, and earn money entertaining tourists in the villages.

The northwestern province of Esmeraldas is extraordinarily green, as its name—meaning "emeralds"—suggests. Heavy rains

61

water the rolling pastures, tropical fruit trees and thick forests. The first Spaniards to arrive here found large settlements along the Esmeraldas coast, and they were met by thousands of warriors. Later, a Spanish ship carrying Black slaves from Africa was wrecked here. Then many more Black slaves filtered down from Colombia. Gradually, the Black population of Esmeraldas increased and the native Indian population became smaller. The races fought to begin with, and then intermarried, producing *zambos* (Black-Indian mixture), and *mulattos* (Black-White mixture).

There are still over three thousand Cayapa Indians in Esmeraldas. Most of them live along rivers in the northern part of the province, where they are being surrounded by lumber companies cutting down the forest. The Cayapas fish, farm and hunt, using

A Colorado Indian in Santo Domingo de los Colorados. *Colorado* in Spanish means "red"—the Indians were given this name because of the red vegetable dye with which they decorate their bodies.

magnificent canoes for travelling. But they are losing their language and traditions as *mestizos* and *mulattos* move into the area.

A fabulous treasure island, called La Tolita, lies just off the northern coast. It was discovered and sacked by treasure-hunters many years ago, making it practically impossible for modern archaeologists to do any proper investigation. Enormous quantities of gold were taken from La Tolita, and much of the finest jewelry was melted down for sale. Hardly any ceramic figures were left unbroken as a result of the pillage. One magnificent gold and platinum mask has survived, and is in Quito's Central Bank museum. About two thousand years ago there seems to have been a large population on the island. From the quantity of gold, it seems both rich and poor wore gold ornaments, and many people were involved in making them.

The city of Esmeraldas is a chaotic place. It has a busy fishing-port and modern cargo wharf, as well as sawmills and small boat-building yards. Lumber, cocoa and bananas are brought down the Esmeraldas River on rafts or canoes for export. Shacks grow higgledy-piggledy along the river banks and up the hills behind the city. Southward along the coast, long white beaches backed by palm trees attract Quiteños. People enjoy fried fish, crabs and shrimp in the beachfront restaurants, and the local music has African rhythms.

Esmeraldas is the terminal for the oil pipeline from the Amazon region. Crude oil is piped out to tankers that wait offshore. Ecuador's largest oil refinery is just outside the city, and estates have been built near by to house those who work for the state oil company. The refined products, such as petrol, are transported back

A gold mask found on the island of La Tolita. This is now in Quito's Central Bank museum.

to inland cities for sale.

Although many of the people who live in the coastal lowlands originally came from the highlands, they consider themselves quite different. The machete-carrying peasant on the coast is supposed to be more independent and rebellious than the highlander. Guayaquileños say they work harder than Quiteños, and that Guayaquil is the engine that pulls Ecuador along.

7

The Galápagos Islands

Giant tortoises—called *galápagos* in Spanish—may weigh as much as a quarter of a ton and live for 150 years. They can survive for months without food and water, and this allows them to last through long droughts. Unfortunately, this characteristic also made them very useful to the pirates and whaling-boats that used to stop off in the Galápagos Islands. Tens of thousands of tortoises were stacked in the holds of such ships, and kept alive. They provided fresh meat and good oil on long sea voyages.

The first European to discover the islands and describe the extraordinary tortoises was Tomás de Berlanga, Bishop of Panama. His ship was carried westward from the coast of South America, and he landed on the Galápagos in 1535. Nobody took much interest in the curious craggy islands for another 150 years, when pirates began raiding Spanish ships and towns along the Pacific mainland. The Galápagos Islands made an ideal base for the pirates. They found shelter, food and water there within easy reach of their prey. One favorite pirate anchorage is now called Buccaneer Cove.

After the pirates came the whalers. They chased whales migrating north from Antarctica to the equator. Thousands of Galápagos fur seals were also killed in the islands, because their pelts were so valuable. The whaling crews took tortoises and any other provisions that could be found on the inhospitable islands. During this period, someone built a post-box on Floreana island. It was made out of a barrel, and sailors left their letters in it, to be picked up by a ship heading homewards. The barrel is still in use.

Some early visitors recognized that many plants and animals on the Galápagos Islands were unique. But it was not until Charles Darwin put forward his theory of evolution that anyone explained why this should be. Darwin, who was travelling on *HMS Beagle* as the ship's naturalist, stayed in the islands for about five weeks in 1835. He was fascinated by the fact that giant tortoises on different

A tourist taking photographs of a giant tortoise on Santa Cruz.

islands were obviously different from one another, even though all the islands had the same volcanic origin and much the same climate.

Darwin eventually published *Origin of Species* twenty-two years after his Galápagos visit. The islands provided ·evidence for his theory that species are not unchanging living forms, created at a particular moment in time. Instead, they change by "natural selection." The species best suited to the local environment survive and continue to evolve. Giant tortoises became extinct on the mainland, where there was competition from other species. But they thrived in the isolation of the Galápagos.

The differences between the giant tortoises can be explained mostly in terms of climate and vegetation: for example, the high, raised shells and long necks of some giant tortoises make it easier for them to reach out for plants to eat. These are the ones that normally live on smaller, drier islands where vegetation is scarce.

Darwin (and most scientists since) believed that the Galápagos Islands have never been connected to the mainland. They are made almost entirely of basalt lava and rock, thrown up from the ocean floor by volcanic eruptions. Cones, craters, swirling lava fields and jagged black cliffs give the landscape an eerie quality. Earthquakes and spectacular eruptions often shake the islands today. Isabela, the largest island, has five active volcanoes, including Wolf, which rises to 5,577 feet (1,700 meters). There are over six thousand giant tortoises on Isabela; each of the big volcanoes has a different type of tortoise living on its slopes.

Plants and animals could have reached the islands by many routes. Some birds probably flew there direct from Central and

South America. They may have carried seeds in their feathers and on their feet. Other animals drifted across on logs and clumps of vegetation carried along by ocean currents. Seeds could also have been blown by the wind. It would have been difficult for big land mammals to reach the islands in these ways, so the reptiles (including the giant tortoises) have been left in peace.

Although the Galápagos Islands lie on the equator, they do not have a very hot, wet climate. The Humboldt Current cools the air much of the year, and the sky is often overcast. It is hottest from January to April, when there are rain showers. Cold and warm ocean currents mingle in the area, making it possible for both penguins and tropical frigate birds to live on the islands.

As there are long dry periods, the vegetation at low altitudes is

Typical Galápagos scenery. As there are long dry periods, the vegetation at low altitudes is mostly scrubby and thorny.

A land iguana, with a high ridge of spines running the length of its back.

mainly scrubby and thorny. Thickets of small spiny trees and several kinds of cactus sprout out of the broken lava. Mangroves with glossy leaves and tangled roots grow along the shore, especially in sheltered bays. Higher up, it is damper and misty. There are forests of sunflower trees, as well as mosses, vines and shrubs. This is the best farming zone in the islands, and some of the native vegetation has been cut down to plant fruit trees, coffee and sugarcane. Ferns and grasses cover the highest mountain slopes.

Two-thirds of the birds living in the Galápagos Islands are not found anywhere else in the world. Most of them are unusually tame, and will walk right over people's feet. There are bright blue-footed

69

and red-footed booby birds, waved albatrosses, flightless cormorants, Galápagos hawks, and thirteen kinds of finches. Even the iguanas are tame. Land iguanas grow more than three feet (one meter) long and live in dry areas where they can eat cactus and bask in the sun. Some are quite yellow, with a high ridge of spines running down their backs.

Marine iguanas spend a lot of time basking on the rocks too. When swimming, they keep their legs tucked in, and propel themselves with their tails. They live on seaweed, sometimes diving quite deep into the sea to find it. Although marine iguanas are black with long black crests, the males on some islands look reddish at breeding time.

Giant tortoises spend a lot of time eating plants and sleeping. They wallow dozing in muddy ponds in the higher, wetter parts of the islands. But a tortoise can walk at the rate of four miles (six kilometers) a day, and the males become very aggressive during the mating season. The females plod down to the dry zone to lay round white eggs in a small hollow in the ground. It takes about eight months for the eggs to hatch, and the tiny tortoises have to dig their way out through a mud crust.

Many of the tortoises do not survive. Rats eat the eggs, and dogs and vultures attack the young creatures as soon as they emerge. There are now about ten thousand giant tortoises left on the islands, and scientists at the Darwin Research Station are doing their best to protect them. Sometimes eggs are taken to the station for hatching; the young tortoises are returned to their islands when they are big enough to defend themselves. Groups of tortoises are also kept for breeding in a safe environment.

The Darwin Research Station is on Santa Cruz, where the tourist trade is based. Scientists work with the government and with National Park rangers to preserve endangered species and limit the number of visitors to each place. There are guides to stop people straying off the main paths and disturbing nesting animals. The National Park includes nearly all the islands except for farmland. Most people live on San Cristóbal, Santa Cruz and Isabela, but boats take tourists to the smaller islands.

Ecuador formally claimed the Galápagos soon after independence, but at first only a few convicts and eccentrics settled on the islands. During the Second World War the United States built an airbase on Baltra, and there is also an airport on San Cristobal. About ten thousand people live on the Galápagos now. Most of them earn a living from farming, in tourism, or working for the government. Fruit, fish, vegetables and meat are plentiful; nearly everything else needed by residents and visitors has to be shipped out from Guayaquil—and every beer bottle has to go back to the mainland to be filled up again.

Scientific interest and a good tourist income have encouraged the Ecuadorean government to look after the Galápagos. The islands are recognized all over the world as an important part of man's heritage. In the past many native animals were killed; and the ecology of some areas has been upset as a result of introducing new plants. Now the government is trying to prevent any further damage, and is teaching both islanders and tourists to appreciate this unique environment.

71

8

The Amazon

The streams that tumble down Ecuador's eastern mountain ranges turn into broad, muddy rivers on the Amazon lowlands. Eventually, they join the River Amazon itself and flow across the continent to the Atlantic Ocean. Heavy rains in the mountain region can swell the rivers in a few hours, forming torrents that sweep away trees. In the drier season, between December and March, the water often becomes so shallow that canoe travel over the rapids is dangerous.

Soon after the Spaniards founded Quito, they sent off expeditions to explore the Amazon jungles. In 1541 Gonzalo Pizarro (brother of the conquistador Francisco Pizarro) set out over the mountains with more than two hundred Spaniards and four thousand highland Indians. They took horses, weapons, pigs and grain. Struggling through the jungle was more difficult than they expected, and the horses were little use. Some of their supplies were lost one night when a river rose suddenly and washed away the camp. It was not long before sickness weakened the expedition and food ran out, so Pizarro decided Francisco de Orellana should go

Rainforest on the eastern slopes of the Andes.

on downstream to look for provisions.

Pizarro waited in vain for Orellana to return. Orellana and his men, by now practically starving, pushed on down the rivers until they found some well-stocked villages. They had already travelled so far from Pizarro that it seemed best to continue. So they built a bigger boat and sailed on for eight months, becoming the first Spaniards to go all the way down the Amazon.

Neither the Incas nor the Spaniards managed to subdue the fierce Shuar Indians who lived in the southeastern Amazon forests. Twice the Shuar fought off the Inca troops. They rolled huge rocks onto the highlanders as they marched through ravines, and ambushed

73

them. The Incas retreated, deciding it would be better to leave the Amazon people alone.

When the Spaniards advanced down to the lowlands, the Shuar warriors used the same tactics. But the Spaniards were eager for gold, and they were much more persistent than the Incas. New jungle settlements were established, and Indians—some of them brought from the highlands—were forced to pan for gold along the rivers. The Shuar rebelled against this treatment, setting fire to two towns and driving the Spaniards out of their territory. The Spanish governor is said to have paid for his greed by having molten gold poured down his throat.

Although many Amazon Indians were killed in battle, even more died from the European diseases inadvertently brought to the country by the Spaniards. Today, isolated jungle groups are still vulnerable to coughs, colds and chicken-pox. A whole village can be wiped out by a flu or measles epidemic, unless vaccines and medicines arrive in time.

As traders and Catholic missionaries moved further into the Amazon region, most of the Indians fled deep into the forest. But some stayed near the missions founded by the religious orders. They were baptized with Spanish Christian names, and they worked to support the religious communities, building churches and planting crops. Others were put into slavery, carving large farms out of the jungle. The Spaniards saw the Amazon Indians as ignorant savages who had to be converted and civilized. Even today few people try to understand Indian customs, or to take advantage of their knowledge of the forest.

An Amazon Indian man.

During the last part of the nineteenth century, the expansion of the world rubber trade brought more suffering for the Indian population. Traders set up collecting camps along the Amazon tributaries, and shipped cargoes of rubber down to Belém, at the mouth of the Amazon. They sent captured Indians out to draw the sticky latex from rubber trees scattered through the forest. The Indians were often tricked into working for the traders by the promise of good wages. When they got to the camps, they found the wages were too low even to pay for their food. So they stayed in debt to the traders however hard they worked, and many died of the

75

brutal treatment they received in the camps.

There are still about 80,000 Amazon Indians in Ecuador, but nearly all of them have settled in permanent villages. A few remain out of touch—hunting, fishing and gathering plants in the most remote part of the forest. The largest Indian groups are the Quichua and the Shuar. Many tribes shown on old maps have died out completely, while only a few of the Cofan, Huaorani, Siona and Secoya survive today.

For centuries the Indians had enough room to live a semi-nomadic life in the forest, and to farm in their own way. They would cut down enough trees to plant a mixture of crops, such as manioc roots, peanuts, bananas and maize. The men hunted monkeys, birds and other animals with blow-guns and poisoned darts. (The darts are pushed into the end of the blow-gun's long tube, and blown out with a strong puff.) When the animals became scarcer and the crops

A Cófan Indian hut in the Amazon region.

yielded less, the Indians would move on to a new area. The forest grew back quite quickly; it had not been seriously disturbed, and the soil recovered.

So many new colonists are settling in the Amazon lowlands that there is no longer enough land to let the forest grow back. Crops have to be sown again and again on the same piece of land. Even though the jungle vegetation looks so green and luxuriant, the soil is not as rich as it seems. After a few good harvests, fertility is lost and diseases attack the plants. Very large pastures are needed to support only a few cattle. But some permanent crops—for example, fruit trees, cocoa and coffee—do well, especially when they are all grown together.

Colonists who arrive from the crowded highlands take some time to get used to the jungle climate and the insects. They often build their wooden houses on stilts, as the Indians do, to avoid floods and animals. Brightly-colored tropical plants grow near the houses, and there is sometimes a cement floor out in front for drying coffee and cocoa beans.

Several roads now wind down the steep mountain gorges, linking the highlands with Amazon towns such as Puyo, Sucúa and Lago Agrio. Every year more of the forest disappears as cattle ranchers, lumber companies and small farmers advance further eastward from the Andean foothills.

The Amazon region's most important product is oil. In 1972 the trans-Andean pipeline to the coast was finished, and Ecuador began exporting oil from the wells near Lago Agrio. As the state petroleum company and foreign firms explored for more oil, new roads were

Building a road through Ecuador's Amazon lowlands.

built, settlers arrived and the whole area changed. Now people hang clothes to dry on the pipelines, and small planes buzz busily from one oil camp to another.

All these developments have forced change on the Indians too. Since 1991 they have belonged to the Organization of Ecuadorean Achuar Nationalities to try and get land-ownership papers and bank loans to improve their farms. They send representatives to Quito to negotiate with the government for health clinics and schools. The Shuar have a bilingual education system, and broadcast on their own radio in Shuar and Spanish. Teachers out in the forest help the school children follow math and grammar lessons on the radio. Because of this system, they can live at home instead of moving to town to study. Some go on to university, and study subjects that will be useful to the Indian organization. Many of the Indians can see that development is inevitable, and they want to have a share in it; at the same time, they are trying to preserve their own traditions.

9

Natural Resources

Ecuador has an unexpected range of crops and farming systems for a tropical country. Different products are grown at different altitudes, from sea-level to 13,120 feet (4,000 meters); and the varied climate allows some crops to be harvested all the year round. The country produces most of its own food except for wheat, which is imported from the United States. About one third of all employed Ecuadoreans work in agriculture, and it brings in an important share of foreign earnings.

The main export crops are grown in the coastal region. Ecuador has some of the world's best quality cocoa. Part of the harvest is dried and exported as beans, without any processing; but factories around Guayaquil turn some of the beans into cocoa products, which are also exported. Although there are some cocoa plantations, many farmers mix cocoa trees with bananas and coffee. Then if the price of one crop drops when the harvest is ready, the farmer should be able to keep going with the income from the others.

Bananas grow in all the coastal provinces, and in many different

Bananas stacked ready for shipment.

shapes and sizes: the *Orito* is a tiny, sweet banana; the *Cavendish* is the best yielding variety. Galo Plaza, who was president of Ecuador from 1948 to 1952, encouraged foreign companies to invest in banana production when their Central American plantations were ravaged by diseases. Within a few years Ecuador became the world's biggest banana-exporting country.

More than two million tons of bananas are produced in Ecuador each year. The bunches have to be picked while they are still green, so the fruit ripens as it reaches the shops in Europe and elsewhere. As Ecuador is on the west coast of South America, the bananas have to travel a long way to the main markets. The passage through the

Panama Canal also costs extra, making it tough to compete with other countries.

Coffee is another important export crop, but yields are rather low. Sugarcane, cotton, rice and African palm grow well on the lowlands and are needed for local consumption. Occasionally, in a very good year, there is enough left over for export. Farms in the coastal region vary from large commercial plantations with a big labor force, to peasant holdings worked by a family. Some of the cattle ranches are enormous, while small-scale farmers usually keep a few pigs and chickens, as well as a horse.

Highland agriculture is more backward on the whole. Steep mountain slopes make it difficult to use modern machinery, and fields are plowed with oxen. However, the gentler upland valleys shelter big herds of dairy cattle, and some excellent cheeses are produced. One of the chief problems in the *Sierra* is the difference in the size of landholdings. Small farms are over-worked, while big estates may have extensive areas which are not cultivated at all.

Over one quarter of Ecuador's land is still forested, though trees are being cut down at an alarming rate. Good quality lumber is taken from the Amazon region to the highlands for making furniture, for construction, and for processing into plywood. In parts of the highlands, pine forests and eucalyptus trees have been planted to try and control soil erosion on mountainsides. People living in the country need firewood for cooking, and this uses up a lot of trees every year. The province of Esmeraldas has some of the largest forests, but chain-saws and sawmills are eating them up fast. Balsa wood, which is very light and buoyant, is exported from this area.

Thousands of greedy pelicans can always be seen along the Ecuadorean coast—a good advertisement for the fine fishing. The cold Humboldt Current feeds a rich variety of sea life. Another warmer current, called El Niño, flows southward; *el niño* means "the child," and the current usually appears around Christmas when the Christ child was born. Sometimes the currents mingle, and sometimes El Niño pushes the Humboldt Current back; the change in temperature may lead to heavy rains, floods and disastrous fishing for a period.

The main fishing-fleets are based in Manta, Esmeraldas and Guayaquil, though there are fishing-craft all along the coast. The larger boats bring in tunny, mackerel, herring, pilchards and other varieties of fish to be processed for export. Some of the catch is turned into fishmeal for feeding to farm animals, some is canned, and the remainder is frozen. Boats from countries such as the United States also come to fish off Ecuador's coast. At times, the tunny shoals seem small and difficult to find. Experts are concerned that fishermen may be taking too much from the sea; experiments in controlling the lobster catch have produced good results.

Shrimp farming has been a major success; most of Ecuador's shrimps are now produced in ponds. Huge ponds stretch along the sandy salt-flats just behind the shore. Tiny shrimp grow into adults within a few months when they are well fed. But the larvae needed for breeding shrimp shelter among the very mangrove trees that are being cut down to make way for more ponds. The government is encouraging people to set up laboratories to produce larvae, so that shrimp exports increase.

Although so many families live from farming and fishing, Ecuador's recent development has been based on its oil wealth. In 1917 a British company began to produce oil in the Santa Elena peninsula, west of Guayaquil. There are still many old wells in the dusty desert landscape, pumping a few barrels a day. The oil is processed in nearby refineries. But the reserves of the Santa Elena fields have practically run out. It is the Amazon region that now produces nearly all the country's oil.

Foreign companies began to explore for oil in the Amazon jungle as early as the 1920s. But the development of the Amazon reserves had to wait until Texaco and Gulf made a series of very successful drillings in the late 1960s. The companies built a 310 mile- (500 kilometer-) long pipeline across the Andes to Esmeraldas, and oil started to flow along it in 1972. Suddenly, Ecuador's export earnings jumped, and in the early 1980s oil provided about two-thirds of

Shrimp-breeding pools near Guayaquil.

Drilling for oil in the Amazon region.

Ecuador's foreign income and today provides 45 percent of Colombia's export income. A second pipeline was more recently built that takes oil directly to Colombia.

Millions of acres of Amazon forest were opened for oil exploration in the mid-1990s with many negative effects on the Indian communities and national parks in that area. Environmental concerns are gradually being addressed and the oil companies are taking more responsibility for the land and its people. Oil is by no means the country's only source of energy. There are large natural gas deposits in the Gulf of Guayaquil, which may lead to the development of petrochemical industries. In addition, the fast-flowing rivers that cut steep canyons on either side of the Andes can generate huge quantities of hydroelectric power. Already dams have been built on two of these rivers, and more are planned.

Surprisingly little is known, however, about Ecuador's mineral resources. Gold and silver were the only metals that interested the Spaniards, and they did not find nearly enough to satisfy them. More gold deposits have been discovered since, especially in the southern province of Loja. People from all parts of the country go there to try their luck, but they have to work hard in miserable conditions. The government is making it more attractive for companies to mine gold with modern equipment, instead of leaving it to prospectors with shovels and wire sieves. There are also deposits of copper, lead, molybdenum (a metal used for strengthening special steels) and zinc to be developed at some time in the future.

10

Food and Drink

Snacks or picnics, festivals or funerals—food and drink are an essential part of every occasion in Ecuador. A funeral without a feast would be an insult to those who attend; and even the poorest home will have something special to serve a visitor. According to Indian tradition, anyone who comes to the house must be offered refreshment.

The Andean highlands are the home of the potato. Soon after the Spanish conquest, potatoes were taken to Europe, and then grown all over the world. But nowhere else are there as many different kinds as in the Andes, from the tiny round yellow ones to the purple-skinned giants. Potatoes are the mainstay of most highland meals, whether boiled or baked, in soups or in stews.

In the old part of Quito, women fry mashed potato cakes stuffed with cheese, called *llapingachos*. Whole roast pigs, with their snouts resting on the edge of a tin tray are sold on weekends and disappear fast. *Llapingachos*, avocado and roast pork, topped with a hot red pepper sauce, make a favorite Sunday lunch.

A tasty snack of roast pork in Saquisilí market.

Out in the countryside people are more likely to eat guinea pig (*cuy*), cooked on a spit over an open fire. Highland Indian families often have dozens of squeaking *cuys* running round on the earth floor of the kitchen. They pick up scraps to eat, and breed so fast that there are always a few plump ones ready for a special occasion.

Markets are a popular place for a snack—or even a substantial meal of chicken soup and lamb stew. Highland Indians carry most of their shopping on their backs, so their hands are free to pick up tidbits which they munch along the way. Maize is eaten in every form imaginable: corn on the cob with a slice of cheese, crunchy toasted kernels, handfuls of boiled maize or *mote,* and ground sweet-maize cakes wrapped in banana leaves. *Empanadas* (the local version

87

Mounds of vegetables on sale in Saquisilí market.

of cornish pasties) and *patacones* (crisp-fried banana slices) also make good snacks.

The mounds of fruit and vegetables in the markets are always tantalizing. Many are grown all year round, because there is so little variation in temperature near the equator. Instead, temperature changes according to altitude, so lowland tropical fruits are taken up to the highland markets, and vice versa. Alongside mountain-grown peaches and blackberries are grapefruit, pawpaw and mangoes from the hot regions. Exotic fruits such as grenadines, guavas and passion-fruit are made into delicious juices and ice creams.

Special foods are often served at certain festivals. On All Saints' and All Souls' days (when people visit graves in the cemeteries) a

88

thick, syrupy drink called *colada morada* is made. *Colada morada* consists of mulberries, strawberries and pineapple mashed up with cloves and cinnamon. Dolls made from sweet bread are eaten with it. At Easter, Ecuadoreans make a rich soup called *fanesca*. All sorts of grains and beans go into fanesca, as well as dried fish, pumpkin, ground peanuts, garlic, cheese and cream.

Chicha, a kind of maize beer, is drunk on most social occasions in the highlands. In the jungle, no meal is complete without large amounts of *chicha*. It is usually made of manioc rather than maize in the lowlands. In the Amazon region, women boil up vast quantities of manioc roots, then chew them and spit the pulp into big jars. The mixture ferments gradually, making a nourishing drink. If the hunters have been unlucky, breakfast and lunch may consist of nothing but *chicha*.

Manioc, sweet potatoes and bananas grow well in the jungle, and are cooked nearly every day. When the rivers are low it is easy to catch fish. Sometimes an Indian community will dam up a stream and kill the fish by poisoning the water with a jungle vine. If plenty of fish are caught, some will be salted or smoked so that they keep longer. The Indians look for turtle eggs in the river banks, but these are becoming as scarce as the trout in mountain lakes. When someone manages to kill a tapir or a large monkey, the whole community has a feast.

Many Ecuadoreans can only afford to eat meat and eggs once in a while. They live mainly on starchy foods, and the children do not grow as strong as they should. Herbs and peppers are often used in the cooking to make grains and root vegetables more interesting; but people eat surprisingly few green vegetables, considering the variety that can be grown.

There are all sorts of seafood dishes in the coastal regions. One of the most popular is *cebiche*–shrimp or fish soaked in lemon juice with onion, and chilled. Ecuadoreans say a *cebiche* and a cold beer make the best cure for a hangover. Rice is served with most meals in the lowlands, and sometimes it is mixed with coconut and fish. A good breakfast for people going out to do a hard day's work would include rice, fried steak with an egg on top, and cooked bananas.

Sweet *cocadas*, made out of coconut, sell well on street stalls, and coconut cake is always appreciated too. At lunchtime women often take saucepans full of food to sell to workers on construction sites. They also set up temporary restaurants in the parks, and offer a cheap plateful of potatoes, rice, broad beans and a small piece of meat. The hot red-pepper sauce is always there to add spice.

In the larger cities, American-style foods such as hamburgers, sodas and chips have gained popularity. There are lots of Chinese restaurants and sandwich bars too. City families may have a *parrillada* (barbecue) in the garden on Sundays, and eat roast turkey at Christmas. But in the rural areas eating habits are much slower to change, and people depend on what they can produce. Many of today's foods–maize, potatoes, beans, peppers–were grown in pre-Spanish times. Although the old cooking-pots have been replaced by aluminum saucepans, most country cooking is still done in a rough stone open fireplace.

11

Fun and Fiestas

Ecuadoreans seem to spend much of the year getting over one *fiesta* (festival) and preparing for the next. *Fiestas* are an important part of life, especially in the countryside where traditions are strongest. Before the Spaniards arrived *fiestas* were closely linked to the seasons, and to the worship of the sun and the moon. The Incas celebrated *Inti Raymi*, the feast of the sun, at the end of June, when the maize and potato harvests had been brought in. They offered sacrifices to the sun, and the ceremonies were followed by feasting and dancing.

Although the Catholic Spaniards were shocked by "pagan" Inca festivals, they managed to take advantage of them. Saints' images replaced those of the ancient gods, and the Indians became Catholics; even so, the priests allowed many traditions to continue, making it easier for the Indians to accept their new religion.

June is still a *fiesta*-filled month in the highlands. Several Catholic feast-days coincide with the harvest period, and in some villages the drinking and dancing may go on for two weeks. During Corpus

Dancers at the Corpus Christi fiesta in Cañar.

Christi dancers wear very elaborate costumes, colorfully embroidered and sewn all over with coins. Their enormous head-dresses are studded with mirrors, jewelry and small figures, and bunches of feathers stick out at the top.

Organizing a highland *fiesta* is a major task. Several months in advance the village community decides who will act as the sponsor. It must be somebody who can get together the dancers, costumes, fireworks and a lively band, as well as plenty of food and drink. If the *fiesta* is a success, the sponsor and his family will be very well thought of. The *fiesta* always includes at least one mass in the church, and a procession around the village square, led by the priest and the dancers.

Holidays for the feast-days of Saint John, Saint Peter and Saint Paul follow soon after Corpus Christi. All through this time the villagers are enjoying parties, visiting one house and then another. People often wear masks and speak in high squeaky voices to try and disguise themselves. There is always somebody who plays a musical instrument in the group, and each family provides enough refreshment to keep everyone dancing. Towards the end of the *fiesta*, more and more revellers fall in a heap by the wayside to sleep it all off.

Easter celebrations start with Palm Sunday, when people take palm leaves into the churches and have them blessed by the priest. During Holy Week the churches are crowded, and religious images are prepared for the processions. On Good Friday a huge procession winds through the old streets of Quito. Wearing purple robes and tall, pointed hoods, the penitents accompany the image of Jesus around the city. Thousands of people follow, some dressed as Roman soldiers, some carrying heavy crosses, and a few beating themselves in punishment for their sins.

All Souls'—the Day of the Dead—is not as depressing as it sounds. Visiting the dead, and sitting by their graves in the cemeteries, is another occasion for a *fiesta*. Families go together, taking flowers, gilded cards, and food and drink as gifts for the dead. In both towns and villages, the cemeteries are full of people cleaning and decorating graves, sometimes even having a picnic alongside the headstone.

Although most *fiestas* are linked to religious holidays and saints' days, a new bus service or community center can provide the excuse just as well. Sometimes there may be improvised bullfights. Villagers jump into the ring and wave their ponchos at the bulls—luckily the bulls are not usually very fierce. One favorite *fiesta* game is the greasy pole, with competitions to see who can climb to the top first.

Anniversaries are also a good time for celebrations. Big parades along city avenues commemorate independence and foundation dates. Quito enjoys a whole week of revelry up to December 6, with bullfights, exhibitions, and dancing in the streets. At Ambato's fruit and flower festival during Carnival, exotic floats topped by smiling beauty queens dazzle visitors from all over Ecuador. It is a welcome escape from Carnival elsewhere, which consists of hurling water at

Quito cemetery, on All Souls' Day.

friends and passersby. On the coast, frenzied water battles go on for several days.

At Christmas, children help make nativity scenes showing the birth of Jesus. In some places there are processions; in others people re-create the events of Christmas Eve in Bethlehem, with adults, children and animals dressing up to take part in the play. New Years's Eve is a big *fiesta* for children too. Girls dress up in black, as the widows of the old year. Neighbors get together and build comic tableaux on street corners, stuffing old clothes to make life-size figures. They often represent politicians and people who have been in the news. At midnight all the figures connected with the old year are burnt, and everyone celebrates the new year.

No *fiesta* is complete without music. In the highlands there are all sorts of flutes and string instruments, as well as drums, conch shells, long curling horns and pan-pipes. A noisy brass band is always appreciated too. On the coast around Esmeraldas, black people play music with strong African rhythms, and the older women chant songs about the past. The main instrument is the *marimba*, a xylophone made of wood and bamboo which hangs from a beam. There are also several different kinds of drums and maracas. The *marimba* music is very lively and encourages everyone to dance until they drop with exhaustion.

In the cities traditional *fiestas* are dying out, to be replaced by television, rock music and sports. Ecuadoreans are very enthusiastic soccer and volleyball players. Every village, from the Galápagos to the Amazon, seems to have a net permanently strung up ready for a volleyball game. People often play three-a-side, which makes it even

A village band in procession at a fiesta.

more strenuous. As for soccer, an impromptu game can be played in any street, park or back garden. Local teams compete against each other at weekends on rough village soccer fields, or in the city stadium. Other sports, such as golf, mountain climbing, tennis and swimming, are gradually becoming more popular too.

People living in cities are quick to pick up fashions from North America and Europe, partly because so many foreign television programs are shown. But some Ecuadoreans are interested in keeping cultural traditions alive—and not just for the benefit of tourists. The young Otavalo Indians who have started up music and dance groups hope to strengthen their own identity, as well as entertain others.

12

Looking Ahead

One of the most significant changes in Ecuador over the last twenty years has been the flood of people into the cities. Generally, Ecuadoreans leave the countryside because it is hard to earn a living there, and they believe cities have much more to offer: good schools for their children, a more exciting life, easier work for better wages.

Education is one of the main reasons for moving to cities. Most

Indian schoolchildren. Although many rural areas are still poor, free State primary education is expanding in Ecuador.

migrants have very little schooling, and some cannot read and write. They have to take the lowest-paid jobs—women often work as part-time maids, or collect old newspapers to resell. They are anxious for their children to have a better chance in life.

Families living in rural areas are usually within reach of a primary school—even if it is a long walk to get there. But many of the primary schools are small, with only one or two teachers to take care of all six classes. Sometimes the primary school does not even go as far as the top class, and there is no secondary school.

Although State education is free, books, pencils and other extras have to be paid for. It becomes quite expensive for a poor family to buy good shoes for several children so that they can go to school. The problem is worse in the countryside, as families generally live off the food they can grow, and they have hardly any money.

In the cities, primary schools are better equipped and there is a greater choice. There are many more secondary schools, too, with classes at different times of day. Many of the public secondary schools are seriously overcrowded and those who can possibly afford it send their children to the more elite private institutions.

University education has been expanding fast, and the State universities in the main cities are bursting with students. Although there are practical courses, such as petroleum engineering and agronomy, so many students take law and more general subjects that they find it hard to get jobs. Qualified people—even doctors and teachers—often refuse to go and work in isolated country areas where they are most needed.

The growth in urban population puts great strain on city services and food supplies. Ecuador still has a high birth-rate, and agricultural production has not been rising fast enough to feed everyone. As a result, the country has to import vast quantities of grain. Recently, governments have been investing in programs to improve food production and rural living standards so that people will stay in the countryside.

The rural development programs include building irrigation canals and primary schools, as well as giving bank loans to farmers. Government agronomists advise farmers on what crops to plant, and help them to get seeds and fertilizers.

One of the main problems is transporting food products directly to the cities, avoiding all the traders along the way who raise prices.

Organizations such as the World Bank help finance these programs. Some countries give government aid and send experts to do technical studies or teach new skills. Specialists from the United Kingdom have worked with Ecuadoreans to produce geological maps and to find ways of controlling cocoa diseases. Foreign companies also invest in businesses that look profitable—for example, pharmaceutical plants, oil exploration and shrimp-ponds.

However, Ecuador has to find most of the money for its own development programs. This is particularly difficult when the world prices of the country's main exports—oil, bananas, cocoa and seafood—fall very low. It means borrowing from foreign banks, and spending as little as possible on imports. Prohibiting imports of expensive cars is easy, but local industries need imported materials, such as steel, in order to keep producing.

Ecuador's main foreign trading partner is the United States, and professionals often go to the States to finish their training. A lot of young people learn to speak English, and hope to travel to North America one day. They see it as the new "El Dorado." But others—especially university students—are quite anti-American, and protest about United States' influence.

Ecuador has close ties with other Andean countries, and belongs to South American trading-groups. It also joined the Organization of Petroleum-Exporting Countries soon after oil exports started. Many international meetings are now held in Quito, while Ecuadoreans see more foreign television and travel further. Although country traditions seem to have changed little over the centuries, people in cities are becoming much more outward-looking.

GLOSSARY

conquistadors   Spanish conquerors.

Corpus Christi   Catholic feast day that takes place on the Thursday after the feast of the Holy Trinity (Holy Trinity is on the first Sunday after Pentecost).

El Niño   Warm ocean current that affects Ecuador's weather.

galápagos   Giant tortoises.

hacienda   A large house with much land.

Humboldt Current   Cold ocean current in the Ecuadorian ocean.

iguanos   Large herbivorous lizards.

manioc   Plant that is grown in the tropics for its fleshy edible rootstock.

páramo   Cold grasslands above 13,123 feet (4,000 meters).

Quichua   Native Indian language dating from the Incas still used in Ecuador today.

shoals   A sandbar that makes the water shallow.

tapir   Nocturnal animals that live in tropical climates that have a snout and upper lip that form a long nose.

INDEX

103